Let's Build a Farm

Lisa J. Amstutz

A Division of
Carson Dellosa Education

rourkeeducationalmedia.com

ROURKE'S
SCHOOL to HOME
CONNECTIONS
BEFORE AND DURING READING ACTIVITIES

Before Reading: *Building Background Knowledge and Vocabulary*

Building background knowledge can help children process new information and build upon what they already know. Before reading a book, it is important to tap into what children already know about the topic. This will help them develop their vocabulary and increase their reading comprehension.

Questions and Activities to Build Background Knowledge:

1. Look at the front cover of the book and read the title. What do you think this book will be about?
2. What do you already know about this topic?
3. Take a book walk and skim the pages. Look at the table of contents, photographs, captions, and bold words. Did these text features give you any information or predictions about what you will read in this book?

Vocabulary: *Vocabulary Is Key to Reading Comprehension*

Use the following directions to prompt a conversation about each word.
*   Read the vocabulary words.
*   What comes to mind when you see each word?
*   What do you think each word means?

> **Vocabulary Words:**
> * *harvest*
> * *pipes*
> * *silos*
> * *till*

During Reading: *Reading for Meaning and Understanding*

To achieve deep comprehension of a book, children are encouraged to use close reading strategies. During reading, it is important to have children stop and make connections. These connections result in deeper analysis and understanding of a book.

 ## Close Reading a Text

During reading, have children stop and talk about the following:
*   Any confusing parts
*   Any unknown words
*   Text to text, text to self, text to world connections
*   The main idea in each chapter or heading

Encourage children to use context clues to determine the meaning of any unknown words. These strategies will help children learn to analyze the text more thoroughly as they read.

When you are finished reading this book, turn to the last page for an **After Reading Activity**.

Table of Contents

From Land to Farmland

We need food. Where will it grow?

A farm! Farmers turn land
into farmland.

5

They clear the land of weeds and brush.

They move rocks.

Ready to Plant

Farmers **till** the soil. Soil is the dirt that plants grow in.

Farmers put seeds in the soil. They use a planter.

Pipes carry water to the seeds. *Drip!*

Up, up, up! Plants stretch for the sun.

Farmers watch for weeds and pests.

Now the crop is ripe.

It is time to **harvest**!

Farm Buildings

Farms have buildings. Grain is stored in **silos**.

Tractors and tools are stored in sheds.

Farmers put hay and straw in barns.

Farm animals live in barns too.

Farmers build fences to keep animals safe.

Farmers are busy builders!

Photo Glossary

harvest (HAHR-vist): To gather crops that are ripe.

pipes (pipes): Tubes used to carry a liquid or a gas.

silos (SYE-lohz): Tall round towers used to store grain and other farm products.

till (til): To dig up and prepare land for growing crops.

Plant a Windowsill Herb Garden

It doesn't take much space to grow herbs—just a sunny windowsill. Herbs are fun to grow and taste good, too!

Supplies

three small pots
potting soil
herb seeds—try basil, cilantro, dill, oregano, rosemary, sage, or thyme

Directions

1. Fill the pots with potting soil. Leave about one inch (2.5 centimeters) of space at the top.
2. Place three seeds in each pot. Press them lightly into the soil.
3. Water the seeds. Set the pots in a sunny window.
4. Check your pots every day. Keep the soil moist. The seeds should sprout in a few days.

Index

About the Author

Lisa J. Amstutz is the author of more than 100 children's books. She loves learning about science and sharing fun facts with kids. Lisa lives on a small farm with her family, two goats, a flock of chickens, and a dog named Daisy.

After Reading Activity

Do you like tacos, spaghetti, or salad? Look at the ingredients that go into your favorite meal. How many of them were grown on a farm?

Library of Congress PCN Data

Let's Build a Farm / Lisa J. Amstutz
(My Life Science Library)
ISBN 978-1-73161-504-6 (hard cover)(alk. paper)
ISBN 978-1-73161-311-0 (soft cover)
ISBN 978-1-73161-609-8 (e-Book)
ISBN 978-1-73161-714-9 (e-Pub)
Library of Congress Control Number: 2019932047

Rourke Educational Media
Printed in the United States of America,
North Mankato, Minnesota

Edited by: Kim Thompson
Produced by Blue Door Education for Rourke Educational Media.
Cover and interior design by: Nicola Stratford

Photo Credits: Cover logo: frog © Eric Phol, test tube © Sergey Lazarev, cover tab art © siridhata, cover photo © MaxyM, cover title art © sodesignby, page background art © Zaie; page 4-5 © TDKvisuals; page 6 © AllaSaa; page 7 © kemdim; page 8-9 © B Brown (editorial use only); page 10 © Fotokostic; page 11 © Torychemistry; page 12 © gerasimov_foto_174; page 13 © Olena Mykhaylova; page 14-15 © smereka; page 16 © Sue Smith; page 17 © Sergiy1975; page 18 © Melanie Hobson; page 19 © julie deshaies; page 20-21 © Helen's Photos   All images from Shutterstock.com